Franklin Wells and
R. J. Vaughn was wounded
And Michages Miles miser—
The 3 morning we went back
in town and laid in a line
of battel all day in the Streets
And Ther was a great deel of
fiting don that day but our
division was not could on
The next morning about a hour
befour day we went back about
a mile from town and staid
ther all day
And the morning of The 5 we
left befour day and it a raining
as hard as it could poor and
marched in The direction
of Hagerdstown
but a bout 6
for the yankies
runing up a

D1300567

Malone, Bartlett Yancey

The Reis Library
Allegheny College

Bought from

The Lewis Walker III Memorial

Civil War Book Fund

WITHDRAWN

WITHDRAWN

THE DIARY OF
BARTLETT YANCEY MALONE

Bartlett Yancey Malone

973.782
M297wa

Whipt 'em Everytime

THE DIARY OF
BARTLETT YANCEY MALONE
Co. H 6th N. C. Regiment

Edited by
William Whatley Pierson, Jr.

General Editor
Bell Irvin Wiley

McCowat-Mercer Press, Inc.
Monographs, Sources and Reprints in Southern History
Jackson, Tennessee

1960

Copyright 1960 by McCowat-Mercer Press, Inc.

Library of Congress Catalog Card
No. 60-12635

MANUFACTURED IN THE U.S.A.
by
McCOWAT-MERCER PRESS, INC.
Jackson, Tennessee

CONTENTS

ALLEGHENY COLLEGE LIBRARY

CONTENTS

LIST OF ILLUSTRATIONS

FOREWORD

One of the most remarkable accounts which came to my attention during the research for *The Life of Johnny Reb* was *The Diary of Bartlett Yancey Malone*, rustic young Tar Heel who served in the ranks of the Sixth North Carolina Infantry, Army of Northern Virginia. Malone's diary is remarkable for several reasons. The spelling is refreshingly quaint: Gettysburg is *Gatersburg*; Blue Ridge is *Blew Ridg*; bean soup is *Been Soup*; adjutant is *adjertent*; bloody is *bludy*; some is *sum*; know is *no*; passing through is *passen threw*; peace is *peas*; tunnel is *turnel*; and missing is *misen*. Rapidan appears both as *Rapadan* and *Rappidan*; but difficult words such as Culpeper and Rappahannock are spelled correctly.

The spelling, interesting enough in itself, is the more important for the light it throws on pronunciation; for Malone, like most of the common soldiers, spelled phonetically. Among rural Confederates, as among many of their descendants, a cold day was a *coal day*; closer was *closter*; a court house was a *coat house*; where was *whar*; pretty was *pritty*; Yorktown was *Yolk Town*; until was *untell*; accidentally was *axidently*; ford was *foad*; and verbs frequently were prefixed by the indefinite article as "the Yankies was arunning." Other speech characteristics

11

which have a familiar ring to people who grew up in the rural South are exemplified by Malone's use of "a right smart force," of Federals, "we taken the turnpike," and "we will have a fight hear to reckly"—i.e. directly. Persons interested in orthography and phraseology, and especially the persistence in America of forms common in medieval England can find much that is interesting and revealing in Malone's simple narrative.

Another remarkable feature of this diary is its richness in detail. Douglas S. Freeman noted appreciatively Malone's comments on the weather. But this is only one of many subjects concerning which the diary gives precise and valuable information. His habit of recording the texts used by chaplains and visiting ministers to whom he listened enables the historian to follow the pattern of camp sermons. His notation of distances covered and towns traversed permits an accurate charting of the march of Malone and his regiment to Pennsylvania and back. A verbatim report of a conversation between two Negro guards at Point Lookout, and of the statement of a colored soldier after killing a comrade while "plaing bayonets" with cocked guns ("Jim, Jim, get up from dar, you are not hurt your just trying to fool me"), gives revealing insight into a relatively obscure phase of Civil War history.

Still another remarkable quality of Malone's account is its honesty. This humble Tar Heel was obviously a man of integrity, writing without any thought of publication, but jotting down his experiences for his own information and diversion. What he writes of his observations and experiences is thoroughly credible. There is no basis for doubting him when he tells of a Yankee soldier at Point Lookout shooting a Confederate officer for "jawing" him; of a guard killing a prisoner for peeping through a crack in the wall; of prison fare being unsavory and skimpy; of prisoners freezing; of Rebel inmates stealing from each other and from their Negro keepers; and of a colored sentinel killing a prisoner for "no reason atall." So valuable, indeed, is the detail on prison life that this portion alone would justify republication of the diary.

The value of the new edition is considerably enhanced by the fact that the text of it was carefully checked against the original manuscript—a procedure that was not followed in the first edition for reasons given by Dean Pierson in his new introduction. Another added feature worthy of note is the inclusion of photographs of Malone and some of his fellow Confederates.

BELL IRVIN WILEY

Editors and publisher are indebted to Mrs. Jennelyn Perkins for her enthusiastic and capable assistance with the new edition, and especially for preparing the unique index which retains much of the flavor of Malone's distinctive grammar and spelling.

PREFACE TO THE NEW EDITION

In 1919, *The Diary of Bartlett Yancey Malone* was published at Chapel Hill by the University of North Carolina in "The James Sprunt Historical Publications," Volume XVI, Number 2. It is now republished after having been long "off print" and unavailable to those wishing to obtain a copy through direct purchase. Today, *The Diary,* under new title, format and imprint, is reissued, with the approving consent of the Director of the University of North Carolina Press and the Editor of "The James Sprunt Studies in History and Political Science," to give the present designation of the serial journal in which it originally appeared.

Personally, I am very happy that the Malone diary will again be made available as one of the centennial publications relating to the great war. I have all along thought of the curious document as good reading. The quaintness of expression, the variable phonetic spellings, the occasional indulgence in poetic quotation or composition, the collection of favorite proverbs, the absence of angry bitterness and the unpretentious sincerity and courage of the writer have a charm that endures after many readings. I believe that every year since the diary became "off print" I have received letters of inquiry from persons

15

ALLEGHENY COLLEGE LIBRARY

seeking to obtain a copy. Such letters came from people of diverse interests. Some were students of dialect and language use; some were military historians seeking to consult it for information about weather conditions in some battle or in some sector within the zone of battle. Dr. Douglas Southall Freeman in his *R. E. Lee—a Biography* wrote of the diary as being "very useful for its notes on the weather" and in his *Lee's Lieutenants* he stated that Malone "might be termed the unofficial meteorologist of the Army of Northern Virginia." Some others have wanted they said, to study the ideas and impressions of private soldiers and non-commissioned officers such as might be found in the diary of a sincere and truthful man whose recorded thoughts were unaltered by an editor.

After forty years and after hearing many estimates of this diary, I do not think any statement of the "introductory note" should be withdrawn or seriously modified.

At the time of the original publication, a separate statement concerning the provenance of the document and containing acknowledgments was prepared but inadvertently omitted. The diary was brought to the attention of the editors of "The Sprunt" through the kindness of the late Julius Algernon Warren, for many years the Bursar of the University of North Carolina and a close friend of Bartlett Yancey Malone's family. Since I was at the time working on a study of the Joint Committee on the Conduct of the Civil War, I was asked by Dr. J. G. deRoulhac Hamilton, then head of the Department of

History and Government, to edit the typed copy of the manuscript. The manuscript of the diary had been returned, and I did not then have the opportunity to see it. The typed copy had been carefully checked and rechecked so that an accurate copy was thought assured.

Recently I had the pleasant privilege of meeting Mr. and Mrs. Herbert E. Wilkinson in their home at Mebane, N. C. Mrs. Wilkinson is the daughter of Bartlett Yancey Malone. She, with gracious kindness, allowed me to take the manuscript for extended examination, supplied me with certain photographs, and showed me certain family records and newspaper clippings. I was able to obtain some data about Mr. Malone's after-war life. I wish here to acknowledge with appreciation the kindness of Mrs. Wilkinson and also that of Mrs. J. A. Warren, who introduced me to the Wilkinson family. Some other members of the Malone family have, with cooperative interest, searched for photographs and have made them available to me. I am indebted to Mrs. Allen Osborne, of Robersonville, North Carolina, another daughter of Bartlett Yancey Malone, for the picture of him in uniform.

Mrs. Wilkinson's recollections of her father, based upon childhood's deep affection, were stated with careful moderation. Her estimates of her father might be summarized as those of a man of simple tastes, of unassuming manners, and of good humor. She remarked that he always enjoyed jokes and even told those which were at his expense. She remembered a story that on his

17

arrival at his home after four years of war-time experiences on that day of March 5, 1865, he greeted his family, laid down his gun, and disposed of his meager luggage, saying that he would now go to see his sweetheart. This was Mary Frances Compton, who lived nearby. He was to marry Miss Compton on November 15, 1866. I gathered that, after some house construction, Mr. Malone established himself as a farmer and head of a family which eventually numbered ten children. This family resided about four miles from Prospect Hill, Caswell County, in a rural community known as Hyco Creek—a stream that flowed past his home. The post office was Corbett. Malone's life here was quietly uneventful and happy. To him, the war was over, and he rarely talked about it. In later life, he developed tuberculosis, which his family attributed in its beginnings to the exposure he suffered at Point Lookout. He died May 4, 1890.

The diary was written in compact and generally legible script and recorded in three pocket-sized booklets (3 9/16 x 5 9/16 in.), similar to those in which addresses, business accounts, and casual notations are ordinarily entered. One of them, the thickest, was leather bound; the other two were paper bound. The first had apparently been sent home before the termination of the war for "the benefit of his folks." On the fly leaf of it, in a handwriting other than Malone's, are the words: "Money could not buy this book, though it may appear insignificant to any but indulgent parents and fond brothers and sisters." In the last booklet, some entries and accounts were written after Malone's return. One set of these entries, recorded without date, was entitled "Malones Dictionary." Since it has some elements of curiosity, it is reproduced in full in the Appendix.

WILLIAM WHATLEY PIERSON,
Chapel Hill, 1960

Grateful acknowledgement is made to Dr. James W. Patton, Director of the Southern Collection of the University of North Carolina, for his assistance in locating and making available soldiers' photographs contained in the picture section; and to Dr. William Sumner Jenkins, Professor of Political Science, University of North Carolina, for his sustained interest in the diary and his help in microfilming and photostating.

THE DIARY OF
BARTLETT YANCEY MALONE

INTRODUCTORY NOTE

The following is the diary of a North Carolina farmer, Bartlett Yancey Malone, who fought during the American War of Secession from July, 1861, to November, 1863, when he was captured and made prisoner. He entered the Confederate Army at the age of twenty-three as a private and rose to the rank of a sergeant, being a member during his active service of the 6th North Carolina Regiment. As he said, this regiment at the time of his capture in battle on the Rappahannock River belonged to "General Hooks (Hoke) brigard Early Division Ewels Corps Leas Armey." As his story shows, Malone participated in most of the great battles and campaigns in Virginia, Maryland and Pennsylvania. After his capture, November 7, 1863, he was imprisoned at Point Lookout, Maryland, where he remained until February 24th, 1865.

An inquiry as to the justification for the publication of this document would be pertinent, for on a cursory reading it seems little more than an extended weather report. Mr. Malone performed no extraordinary feat of heroism, at least none such was recorded; he participated with individual distinction in no political movement of importance; he played no role which would cause historians to single him out for particular notice. His diary is reproduced here as a document of human interest which reveals, with much quaintness of expression, the thoughts of a simple soldier of the ranks—the thoughts, it is to be presumed, of a mass of men, which have oftentimes been inarticulate. There is a frankness about this diary that conveys inevitably, I believe, the conviction of sincerity. And there is a lack of emotion—as when in remarking on an event which, we are told, caused the soldiers great grief, the death of Stonewall Jackson, he merely said, "And General Jackson died to-day, which is the 10th day of May"—an absence of bitterness and of complaints which, considering the provocation of circumstances, make the diary of almost as much interest because of these omissions as because of what is included. Perhaps the most conspicuously absent feature is that of any statement of the Southern cause for which he was fighting. Not only does the writer refrain from criticism of the North, but he omits to tell why he is fighting for the South. He assumes the Southern cause tacitly and of course, Mr. Malone was chiefly concerned with his job of being a soldier and, as there was no passion nor rancor in his story, there was likewise no exaltation nor fervid declamation. He asserted no particular knowledge of military events nor predicted the result of any engagement. "What the result is to be is more than I no." He did not seem to have been especially elated by victory, and he was certainly not demoralized by defeat—not even that of Gettysburg. He committed himself on rare occasions to expressions which manifested a confidence in the ultimate outcome, as after a successful battle he said: "We whipt them like we aulways do." He was unconsciously a brave man who took a sober sort of joy in fighting. On one occasion, when alluding to a battle of more than four hours in length, which began about three o'clock in the afternoon, he remarked: "we had a wright nice time of it from then on tell dark." There is no notice taken of the horrors of war, of bloody scenes which he must have witnessed on the battlefield; nor were there any complaints made of the pains of the wounds he received. His attitude toward the enemy was unemotional, almost indifferent. He sometimes referred to the federal soldiers as "the Scamps," which, in view of the heated controversies of the time, must certainly be regarded as a mild term of reproach. It is true that he designated General Benjamin F. Butler as the "Yankee beast," but that was an expression then so current in the South as to be conventional so far as Butler was concerned. Having done with these negative, though very significant, aspects, it might be said that, judging from the diary, Malone was chiefly thinking —possibly from a farmer's habit—of the weather with its attendant pleasures and discomforts and about food.

One persistent habit of Malone was to record the texts of sermons which he heard, together with references to their biblical sources. This practice, in addition to revealing some interesting evidence as to the nature of Civil War sermons, will remind some readers of the time when it was considered a cardinal sin to be unable to quote and cite the preacher's text. Religion affected him in this way not only, but it influenced his poetry.

That part of the diary which describes Malone's experience as a prisoner at Point Lookout is, I think, an important and valuable addition to the limited, first-hand material dealing with Southerners in Northern prisons. It was when writing his reflections on prison life that the first note of despair comes into his journals. His criticism of the treatment of prisoners there may be summarized under four heads: First, there was not food enough. "Our rations at Point Lookout was 5 crackers and a cup of coffee for Breakfast. And for a dinner a small ration of meat 2 crackers three potatoes and a cup of soup. Sugar we have non." Later he described the food supplied by saying, "Our Rations gets no better we get half a loaf of bread a day a smal slice of Pork or Beef or Sault Beef for Breakfast for dinner a cup o Been Soup and Supper we get non." Coffee and sugar, which last commodity had for a time been supplied, had been taken away. At one time his friends caught, cooked and ate a rat. Secondly, he wrote of the poor protection against the cold afforded the prisoners. Many had to sleep on the ground with only one blanket. "All the wood we get at Point Lookout is one sholder tirn of pine brush every other day for a tent. 16 men to every tent." He recorded that five men froze to death on one night. Thirdly, he mentioned the frequent shooting of prisoners by the guards for trivial reasons.

At one time he states that a prisoner was shot and killed by the guard "for no reason attall." Fourthly, he rather bitterly resented the placing of Negroes as guards over him.

It will seem strange to some that the writer of this diary should have spelled General Lee's name, which undoubtedly was very familiar to him, as "Lea." This spelling of the famous name may be explained by the fact, of which I have been informed, that in Caswell County there were a number of people who spelled their name "Lea," as, indeed, did an officer of Malone's regiment. This and other orthographic curiosities must be considered in the light of the fact that he was a graduate of the "corn field and tobacco patch" university.

No serious editing has been undertaken. Outside of an occasional attempt to indicate in some cases the accurate form of certain proper names and places, the diary has been allowed to stand without comment as written.

WILLIAM WHATLEY PIERSON, JR.

Chapel Hill, N. C., March 25, 1919.

THE DIARY OF
BARTLETT YANCEY MALONE

Bartlett Y. Malone was bornd and raised in North Carolina Caswell County in the Year of our Lord 1838. And was Gradguated in the corn field and tobacco patch: And inlisted in the war June the 18th 1861. And was a member of the Caswell Boys Company which was comanded by Captain Michel (A. A. Mitchell): And was attached to the 6th N. C. Regiment the 9th day of July '61 which was comanded by Colonel Fisher who got kild in the first Manassas Battel which was July 21, 1861. And then was comanded by Colonel W. D. Pender untell the Seven Pines fight which was fought the 30th day of May '61.* And then Colonel W. D. Pender was promoted to Brigadier General. And then Captain I. E. Avry (Avery) of Co. E was promoted to Lieutenant Colonel who was in comand untell about the 10th of October when he was promoted to Colonel and still staid in comand untell the 2th day of July 1863 which was the day the fite was at Gettysburg whar he was kild. And then Lieut: Colonel Webb taken comand.

B. Y. M.

---

*For a history of the Sixth Regiment, see Clark (editor), *North Carolina Regiments, 1861-1865,* Vol. I (1901).

His purposes will ripen fast
Unfolding evry hour
The bud may have a bitter taste
But sweet will be the flower

May your days be days of pleasure
May your nites be nites of rest
May you obtain lifes sweetest pleasure
And then be numbered with the blest.

Whar ere you rome
What ere your lot
Its all I ask
Forget me not.

Remember me when I am gon
Dear friend remember me
And when you bow befour the throne
O then remember me.

You are a charming little dandy
Sweeter than the sweetest candy.

Candy is sweet
It is very clear
But not half so sweet
As you my dear

One day amidst the plas
Where Jesus is within
Is better than ten thousen days
Of pleasure and of Sin

O for grace our hearts to soften
Teach us Lord at length to love
We alas forget too often
What a friend we have above.

———

All I like of being a Whale
Is a water Spout and a tail.

———

A certen cewer for the Toothack if the tooth is hollow take a pease of the scale that is on a horses leg and put it in the hollow of the tooth It is a serten cewer so sais J. H. Lyon.

B. Y. M.

CHAPTER I

B. Y. MALONE'S MEMORANDUM
FOR THE YEAR 1862

"The snow was about shoe mouth deep"

The first day of January was a beautyfull day

And William Hester died the last day of Dec. 1861

The 2 day was a beautyfull one and nothing happend of eney interest that day.

The 3 day was also a pritty day.

The 4 day we had a right smart snow and Mr. Compton is at our camp to day on a visit.

The 5th which is the Sabath and ther is a right smart ice on the ground to day And Bethel is a cooking I. H. Jonstons big turkey for dinner.

The 6th day was a very coal one indeed and the snow is about a half of a inch deep on the ground to day and Mr. I. T. Compton left our camp to day for home.

31

The 7th day I was on gard and it was a very coal* day.

The 8th day was also coal and me and Bethel washed our close to day.

The 9th day was a beautyfull And Mr. Thomas Martin arived at our camp today on a visit.

The 10 day was cloudy but not much rain And I wrote a letter to S. F. Compton today.

The 11 day was a very pritty day over head but powerfull muddy under foot. And nothing happend to day worth a naming.

The 12 day which is the Sabath and it is a beautifull sunshiney day And me and Young eat our big oposam today for dinner and indeed it was sum good.

The 13 was a very nice day indeed.

The 14 day the snow was about shoe mouth deep And Mr. Clover and Young and Joshua and my self went a rabbit hunting and caught one squirl And indeed we saw a heep of fun that day.

The 15 day was a very bad day it raind all day and freezed as it fell and at night there was about as much ice on the treese as I ever saw in my life.

The 16 day was a wright warm day and the snow nearley all melted off of the ground by night

---

*The form "coal" seems what was intended. Mr. Malone wrote the letters "o" and "a" so much alike that certainty may not be claimed.

The 17 day was very cool and cloudy

The 18 day was sloppy day And I hird today that peas was made between the North and South and I hird that our men sunk a vessel down on the Potomac last night But indeed I dont beleave a word of it.

The 19 day was a raney one and our Company was on picket gard at Greenwood Church which is in about 9 miles from Pocoquan And Mr. I. F. Richmond arived at our camp to day on a visit.

The 20 day and it is still araning and nothing happend today of any interest

The 21 is cloudy and a raning And I am on gard today at the camp

The 22 was cloudy but no rain

The 23 was cloudy and cool but no rain And thir was hevy canonading down on the Potomac to day

The 24 was cool and cloudy in the morning and in the eavning it was a snowing And Mr. Oliver and Young went to Dumpfreese to day for witnesses for Mr. B. Murphey.

The 25 was a very cool day and Young went back to Dumfrieze to day again for witnes for B. Murphey.

The 26 which was the Sabath was a beautyfull day indeed

The 27 was a warm sunshiney day and we all went out on drill to day for the first time in too months And the Colonel praysed ous all and said that he was glad that we had not forgoten how to drill

The 28th day was cloudy in the morning and clear in the eavning And I hope the Lieutenants get sum logs today to put a flower (floor) in his hous

The 29 was a very pritty warm day, but after night it comenced raning And I was on gard to day And my post was right befour the Colonels house door.

The 30 day was a raney day and nothing happend to day onley me and Marshal Walker was a playing and I hurt my face with a fence rail

The 31 day was cloudy but not much rain And nothing happend today worth a menshionen.

B. Y. Malone.

CHAPTER II

"Whar we was to go too we did not no"

The first day of February was a raney day indeed And nothing happened to day of eney interest

The 2 day which was the Sabath was a very warm day

The 3 day was a very bad day it snowed all day long and at night the snow was about six inches deep

The 4 day was a very nice day over head and the snow melted very fast all day, and we boys saw a heep of fun that day a snow bawling

The 5 day was a very warm sunshiney day and the snow was nearly all melted off of the ground by night And nothing happend to day worth a namen

The 6 day was a very raney one And Lieutenant Lea and Sergeant Couvington and H. Rudd and Mr. Balden all started home to day as recruiting officers.

The 7 day was cold and cloudy And I was on gard to day

The 8 day was very cool And Lieutenant Lea was promoted to Captain And Sergeant Olover promoted to Second Lieutenant to day And Nat Hester promoted to fourth Corporal

The 9 day which was the Sabath was a very pritty day And Thomas Grinsted dide to day he was a private in Captian Leas Company

The 10 day was clear but cool And we went out on drill today for the first time in severl weeks.

The 11 day was a very cool day And me and Cousin Anderson went down to the fourth Alabama Reg in a visit.

The 12 day was a very pritty day indeed and I went to Dumfrieze today and then returned home

The 13th day was a pritty warm sunshiney day And we went on drill twist that day.

The 14th day a wright coal day.

The 15 day was a very bad day indeed it snowed all day long and at night the snow was about 3 inches deep on the ground

The 16th day was a clear day and the snow melted a little And Mr. Luther Rudd dide to day about 8 oclock in the morning

The 17 day was a very bad day it rained all day and friezed as it fell.

The 18 day was cloudy but warm and the ice melted off and I was on gard that day

—From Southern Historical Collection
U. of N. C. Library, Chapel Hill

Captain L. M. Nutt

Perkins

Unidentified

H. St. John Dixon

—From Southern Historical Collection
U. of N. C. Library, Chapel Hill

Alexander H. Shotwell

W. H. Fisher

—From Southern Historical Collection
U. of N. C. Library, Chapel Hill

Battle of Gatersburg
"We couldent see what we was a doing"

41

Unidentified

C.S.A.
3 days after the Surrender
1865

—From Southern Historical Collection
U. of N. C. Library, Chapel Hill

No man is bornd without fatts
Too much of one thing is good for nothing
Cut your coat ovearden to your clauth
All are not saints who go to Chirch
All are not theavs tha dogs bark at
Keep your mouth shut and your eyes open
A clean glove often hids a dirty hand
Seay what is well and do what is better
He that will steal a pin will steal a better thing
Fear no man and do justice to all men
Evry cook praises his own Stew
Before thou marry be sure of a house wherein to tarry
Evry body's buisness is no body's buisness
Do what you aught come what may
Love covers many fatts
The race is not always to the swift nor the battel to the strong
You cannot catch old birds with chaff
A bad workman quarrels with his tools
This is the Sabath and the 13 day of March. 1864 By Malone –

Malone's Favorite Proverbs — *from the Diary*

Malone in Later Life

The 19 day was a very raney day indeed And Mr. I. R. Hester And Calvin Snipes arived at our camp today on a visit

The 20 day was a beautifull day it looked like the spring of the year and Mr. I. R. Moore left our camps today to go home on a furlough

The 21 day was cool and cloudy And thar was a wright smart excitement in camp today It was repoted that the Yankees was a landing at Colchester

The 22 day was cloudy and it rained a little in the morning And Mr. I. R. Hester and N. Snips left our camp today for home

The 23 day was cloudy but not much rain

The 24 day was clear and very windey indeed

The 25 day was clear and cool And A. I. Brincefield started home today on a sick furlough

The 26 day was cloudy but not much rain

The 27 day was clear and Brother Albert arrived at our camps today on a visit

The 28 day was clear but very windey and cool And thar was a wright smart stir in camps today for we had orders to pack our knapsacks and to be ready to march at a moments warning but whar we was to go too we did not no. Spring is now come.   B. Y. MALONE.

CHAPTER III

"My post was befour the gard house door"

The 1 day of March was clear and very cool And I was on gard in the day but being unwell I got excused from standing after night

The 2 day it snowed tell the snow was about 2 inches on the ground.

The 3 day was cloudy and rained nearley all day

The 4 day was clear and cool and our company was on picket gard today at Greenwood Chirch

The 5 day was cloudy but no rain And Brother Albert left our camps today for home

The 6 day clear in the morning and cloudy in the eavning And snowed a little And we had orders today from General Whiten (W. H. Whiting) to drill twist every day hear after

The 7 day was clear but very cool and we have orders to cook too days rations and be ready to march in the morning but whar we are agoing is more than I no

The 8 day of March was cloudy and cool And our Regiment left camp Fisher today for Camp Barton

The 9 day was clear and warm And we marched about 15 miles to day on toward Camp Barton

The 10 day was cloudy and raining in the morning but no rain in the eavning And we arrived at camp Barton about 3 oclock in the eavning which is about 2 miles west of Frederksburg (Fredericksburg)

The 11 day was a beautyfull warm sunshiney day and we cleaned our streets and struck our tents today

The 12 day was a beautyfull spring day and nothing occurd of eney interest

The 13 day was warm and clear

The 14 day was warm and cloudy but no rain And I was on gard at Camp Barton for the first time.

The 15 day was a very raney day indeed

The 16 day which was the Sabath was cloudy but no rain And our recruits got in today and the number of them was 45

The 17 day was cool and cloudy but no rain and I hurd today that we had to march back to Richmond

The 18 day was clear and warm And Lieutenant Colonel Lightfoot of the 6th N. C. S. T. was promoted to Colonel of the 5th Alabama Regt today

The 19 day was cloudy and cool

The 20 day was raney and very cool indeed

47

The 21 day cloudy and cool but no rain

The 22 day cloudy and sum rain And I was on gard and the counter sign was York Town

The 23 day which was the Sabath was a beautyfull spring day and I went to Frederksburg to preaching And the preachers text was in St. John 3 chap and 18 virse

The 23 day cool and cloudy

The 24 cool and cloudy

The 25 was a beautyfull day

The 26 was also a nice day

The 27 warm and clear

The 28 was a beautyfull spring day and we have orders this eavning to cook 3 days rashers And I hird severl cannons fyering this eavning but what is to be the result is more than I no

The 29 day it raind and haild and snowed and sleated and friezed and done a little of all that was bad And me and James Colmond went to Fredreksburg and went down to the landing and went in a steam boat for the first one we ever was in

The 30 day which was the Sabath was cool and raney

The 31 day was a beautyfull day and I was on gard and my post was befour the gard house door so nothing more.

B. Y. MALONE

CHAPTER IV

"Yolktown whar we stopt to wait for the Battle"

The 6 day of April which was the Sabath was a beautyfull spring day And I went to Fredericksburg to meating and the Preachers text was in the first Book of Kings 18 chapter and 21 virse

The 7 day was a pritty one

The 8 day was cool and raney And our Regiment left Camp Barton in the morning and marched on toward Richmond threw the wind and water and waded the creaks as they went

The 9 was still cool and raney and we continued our march And about 3 o'clock in the eavning as we was marching threw a little Town cauld Balden Green it comenced halen and raining on ous very hard And then it was about 3 miles to the Depot whar we was to take the cars And we all got very wet befour we got thar And then about sundown we got in sum old horse cars and was run to Ashland which was about 22 miles And when we got thar I was wet and nearly frosen And I was on gard and they put me on post wright away and I had to stand 2 hours And it was a snowing a little while I was a standing

The 10 day was cool and cloudy in the morning but cleerd off about twelve and we stade in Town all day

The 11 day was a pritty clear day and we stade in Town untell eavning And in the eavning we went out in the woods about a mile from Town and struck our tents for the night

The 12 day was a very pritty one

The 13 day was also a nice one And William Jeffrus of our Company dide this morning And we had a Preacher to preach in our camp today and his text was in the Second Book of Kings 6 chapter and 15 and 16 and 17 virses.

The 14 of April was a very pritty day And our Regiment left Ashland for Yolktown (Yorktown) And our rought was down by Hanover Coathouse

The Second day we still continued our march And also the 3 and fourth we marched And the 5 day we marched and past threw the town of Williamsburg about 9 o'clock in the morning And about an hour before the sun set we arrived at General Johnston Headquarters which is in about a mile of Yolktown whar we stopt to wait for the Battle.

The 29 day of April was a beautiful day And Calvin Snips got back today from home And the Reverant Mr. Stewart from Alexander preached in our camp this eavning and his text was this: I am the Lord of Host:

CHAPTER V

"We whipt them like we aulways do"

The 2 day of May was a beautyful one And we had orders to leave Yorktown And soon in the morning the wagons was loded and everything sent off but our knapsacks and about 12 o'clock the Artillery was all plast (placed) in a line of battle acrost the field and about dark we was all marched out behind it and Colonel Pender told ous that they expected a large fight the next day and we lade thar in the field all night with our guns by our side And next morning we marched out in the woods And we stade thar untell about 2 o'clock in the night And then we was rousted up and marched about a half a mile and then for sume cause we was stopt and sent back And then about daybreak we started again and taken the same road back that we come down And about 12 oclock we got to Williamsburg and we onley went about 4 miles futher tell we stopt to stay all night And about 4 oclock in the eavning the Yankee Calvry overtaken ours clost to Williamsburg and we had a little brush but our men whipt thirs and we onley lost one kild and 3 or 4 wounded

And we kild 9 of thirs and wounded severl and taken
10 horses And the 5 day was a very raney one indeed
and we was rousted up about 2 oclock in the night and
marched all day threw the mud and water and at night
we arived in about 2 miles of West Point

The 6 day we stade in camp untell about one oclock
And it was repoted that the Yankees was alanding down
at West Point and we was all run out in a file and plast
in a line of battle expecting a fight but did not and about
dark we marched back to our camp and about 8 oclock in
the night we marched about a mile to another plase for
sume cause and then stade thar all night And the next
morning which was the 8 was a beautyful one and the
Yankees was alanding at West Point and about 8 o'clock
we was marched down to the intended battle field And
from that time untell 12 oclock we was a scurmishing and
a running from one place to another hunting the scamps
And in the eavning we marched back in the woods and
stade thar untell about 12 oclock in the night And then
marched about a mile futher back and stad thar all night
And then as soon as day broke we started on our march
again And about 3 oclock in the eavning we got to West
Point coathouse whar we found General Johnston and all
of his men And then we marched about 2 miles futher
and stop for the night

And the 9 day we rested untell about 12 oclock and
then started out on our march again and befour we had
gone a mile we hird that our Cavalry was attacked by the

Yankees And then we had to stop and wate a while but we whipt them like we aulways do And then we marched on but dident git but 3 miles that day And the 10 day we dident march but about a mile for we was expecting the Scamps to attack us but they did not

The 11 day which was the second Sunday in May was a beautyfull day indeed And we rested all day And the Reverant Mr Stewart from Alexander preached to us again today

The 12 day we still stade in camp and Mr. Fossett preached for us today. And his text was in the first of Timothy 2 chapter and 8 virse

The 13 day was clear and warm

The 14 cloudy and a raining

The 15 raney And we left Camp. Road today about 12 oclock and marched on toward Richmond

And the 16 we marched

And the 17 we got to our camp clost to Richmond

The 26 day of May was a nice one but about 12 oclock in the night it comenced raining very hard And about 1 oclock we was rousted up and did expect to attack the Yankees about day but it rained so hard we did not go

And the 27 day it rained till about 10 oclock and then cleard off And about 3 oclock in the eavning the fight comenced down about Hanover Coathouse we surposed but we was not cauld out And I was promoted today to fourth Corporel

The 28 day was clear and about a hour befour the sun set we left our camp And march all night down toward Hanover Coathouse And we past in about three hundred yards of the Yankeys pickets And then we stopt and rested about 3 hours And about 8 oclock the next day we started back and went about 5 or 6 miles and stopt for the night

And the next day we went back in about a mile and a half of Richmond and staid thar all night

And the next morning which was the 30 we left and marched down toward Chickahominy And about three oclock in the eavning we was led in to the Battle field by Colonel Pender And we had a wright nice time of it from then tell dark

CHAPTER VI

"We had a wright warm time of it But we whipt them"

And the next morning which was the first day of June the fight comenced a little before the sun rose And we was plast (placed) in a line of Battle And was expecting to go in to it evry minuet but we staid thar all day and was not cauld on; General Longstreet divishion don the most of the fighting on Sunday And from that time till the 11th we stade in the Swamp down on Chickahominy River

And the 11 day we left Chickahominy And went to Richmond and taken the cars and went to the Junction that night

And the next morning we left thar And about a hour befour the sun set we arived at Linchburg

And the 12 day we stade at Linchburg

And the 13 day we got on the cars about dark and the next morning we found our relief at Sharlottsvill (Charlottesville) which was about 75 miles from Linchburg And we chainged cars at that plase And the 14 day we traveld threw the Mountins And about too hours befour the sun set we got to the little town cauld Staunton And we stade ther tell the 18 And the 18 which was just twelve months from the time I taken the oath we left Staunton And marched about 15 miles wright back the railroad the way we came down And stade all night at a little town cauld Wainsborough (Waynesboro) clost to the Turnel

And the next morning we croust over the Blew ridg and marched to Mitchiners River And staid thar all night And the next morning which was the 20 we taken the cars at Mitchiners River and road up to Sharlottsvill And then taken a railroad thar that went to Gordnesvill And we got to Gordnesvill about 2 oclock in the eavning and we taken the Richmond Railroad thar And road about 25 miles toward Richmond at a station cauld Fredericks-hall And thar we got off

The 21 we stade at Frederickshall

And also the 22 we stade thar

And the 23 we started out again on our march and marched all day long threw the hot sun and dust for it was very hot and dusty the 23 but it raind that night.

And the next day (which was the 24) we still continued our rout and when we stopt for night we was in 6 miles of Ashland

And the 25 we travield all day long and at night we campt a mile west of Ashland

And the 26 we travield sloley down the Chickahom-iny River driving in the pickets as we went

And the 27 we still went on and about 3 oclock in the eavning we come up with the main body of the Yan-kees (at Cold Harbor) and attacked them And from that time untell dark we had a wright warm time of it But we whipt them And in our company A. Burk was kild and A. Tucker and Page was slitley wounded

And the 28 we marched about a mile the other side of the battle field and stade thar all day,

And the 29 we stade at the same place And about 2 oclock in the eavning we had orders to fall in to march but we did not go And as we was stacking our armes again one of Captain Tates men shot another one threw the thigh but it was don axidentley

And the 30 we was rousted up about too oclock in the night and about day break we started out again And crost the Chickahominy River and marched untell we came to the York river Railroad 8 miles below Richmond And then we taken down the Railroad and about 2 hours befour sunset we come to a little creak whar the Yankees had burnt the bridg And left sum of thir peases thar to bumb us so we couldent build the bridge untell they could get thir armey futher along, And we never got the bridge built untell next morning about a half of a hour by sun

CHAPTER VII

"We overtaken the scamps"

And the next morning whitch was the first day of July just twelve months from the time I left home we crost over and about 10 oclock we overtaken the scamps again And they comenced throwing bumbs amung us And we amung them And thar was a very heavey canonading cept up all day And a little befour night the pickets comenced fyring And from that time untell about a hour in the night thar was very hard fiting don indeed And a great meney kild and wounded on boath sids in our company M. Miles L. Smith, B. Murphey, I. Calmond, G Lyons And my self was all hurt

And the next day which was the second was a very rany day indeed And our Regiment moved back in the woods a peas and stade thar all day

And the next day we marched back about three miles toward Richmond and stopt for the night

And the 4 day we marched down on James River about 25 miles from Richmond

And the 5 we stade at the same plase untell sun down And then our Regiment had to go on picket And we marched down in about a mile of the Yankees and sent out our detail

And also the 6 day we was on picket at the same plase

And the 7 day we was releaved about twelve oclock And then we marched back about a mile in the woods

And the 8 we stade thar untell about 4 oclock in the eavning And then we started out for Richmond And we marched untell about 10 oclock in the night and we got as far as White Oak Swamp which was about 10 miles from the plase whar we started

And the 9 day we started again about 4 oclock and we got in about 3 miles of Richmond And then we moved up in about a mile and a half of Richmond and taken up camp and the 11 we got sum flages and put them up And Mr I. H. Compton arrived at our camp today on a viset

And the 12 day we still stade in camp And also the 13 we stade in camp and Mr. I. H. Compton left our camps today for home for him. And we still staid at Richmond untell the 7 of August And then we left thar And marched about four miles toward Ashland And when we stopt it was dark And then our company had to go about 5½ miles futher to stand picket and it was 12 oclock in the knight when we got to the plase whar we was to stand:

And the next morning we was releived and we had to go back to our Regiment again:

And the 9 day we started out again about four oclock in the eavning and marched untell about one oclock in the knight And when we stopt we was about thre miles beyond Ashland which was about 15 miles from the plase whar we started from

And the 10 day we started again about 4 oclock and we went as far as Hanover Junction which was about 6 miles

And the 11 day we started in the morning and marched about 5 miles down clost to a little river and stopt again to take up camp

And the 14 day our Regt left thar and marched up toward Gordensvill And I was not able to go with them so they excused me and started me back to the Hospital clost to Richmond And we had to walk to Hanover Junction which was about 4 miles And we had to stay thar all next day for we could not get eny cars to tak us eney futher

And the 16 day we got on the cars about 8 oclock and got to the Hospital about 11 And then I staid at the Hospital untell the 2 day of September And then I taken the cars at Richmond and got as far as Gordensvill the first day

And the 3 day we rode on the cars as far as Rapadan River and Bridg was burnt thar and then we had to walk

from thar to our Regiment And it was 115 miles to Winchester And 35 from thar to the Reg. but we left Rapadan the 4 day and walked up the railroad to Culpeper
Coathouse which was 12 miles from Rapadan River

And the 5 day we taken the turnpike road and
marched as far as Warrenton Springs which was 18 miles
from Culpeper

And the 6 day we got to Warrenton about 12 oclock
which was 7 miles from Warrenton Springs And by nite
we got to a littel Town by the name of Baultimore And
it was 5 miles from Warrenton

And the 7 day we got to a little town by the name of
Haymarket about 12 oclock And we dident get but about
4 miles futher that day for we had to stop to get somp-
thing to eat

And the 8 day we got as far as Aldie and it was about
15 miles from Haymarket

And the 9 day we got to Leasburg and it was about 12
miles from Aldie

And the 10 day we past threw a littel town by the
name of Hamelton and it was about 5 miles west of Leasburg And the 11 day we got to Snigerville about nite and
it was 10 miles from Hamilton.

And the 12 day we crost over the Blew ridge in the
morning and about 10 oclock we crost Shandal River and
it was about 4 miles from Snigersville And by nite we
got to Berrysville and it was 5½ miles from Shanandoah

And the 13 day we got to Windchester and it was about 10 miles from Berryville

And then we stade at Windchester untell the 16 and then we started to Harpersferry and we got as far as Berryville the first day and then taken the left hand road and got as far as Charlestown the 17 day

And the 18 day we crost the Potomac at Shepards town about nite and it was 24 miles from Berryville

And the 19 day we crost back again and got as far as Charlestown by night and the 20 day we got to Berryville again

And the 21 we travaild untell we got in 4 miles of Windchester and then taken the wright hand road to go to Martinsburg and we past by the Burnt Factory and got as far as Jordons Sulphur Springs by night.

And the 22 day we got to a littel town by the name of Bucktown and the 23 day we got to our Reg. and it was clost to Martinsburg and Martinsburg was about 22 miles from Windchester

And then the 27 the Regiment left thar and marched in five miles of Windchester

The 22 of October was cool and very windy indeed and the 23 was clear and cool and we had a General revew

And the 24 we left our old camp and marched about a mile near to Windchester to pease of woods and taken camps in them again

63

And the 28 we left thar for Culpeper and got as far as Shanadoah River the first day

And the 30 day the fields was white with froust and about sun up we waded the River at Front Royal and by night we got as far as a littel town by the name of Flint Hill

And the 31 day we marched all day and got in five miles of Culpeper by nite

CHAPTER VIII

"We had to bild ous sum brest works"

And the first day of November we got to Culpeper

And the second day which was the sabath I went to meating at Culpeper And the preachers text was in St: John 16 chapter 7.8.9.10 and 11 virses

And the 3 day we marched over to the old battel field at Sedar Run which was about 3 miles from Culpeper and stopt again for camp

And the 7 day it snowed

And the 8 day the Second and 11 Myssissippians left our Bregaid and the 54 and 57 N. C. taken thir plases

And the 9 day was a very cool day

And the 10 day was a pritty one indeed and thar was a very hevy canonading cept up all day sum whar between Culpeper and Windchester and we had orders to cook rashions and expected to be cauld on evry minnet but was not

And the 18 day we left Culpeper for Fredericks and the first day we was as far as Rapidan River by nite and we marched all day threw the rain and mud the 20 and also the 21 and the 22 we got to Fredericks about 12 o'clock

And the 5 day of December it raind all day and about night it comenced snowing and snowed untell it was about a inch and a half deep on the ground And the 6 day and 7 was very cool indeed

And the 11 day the too signerl guns was fyerd just befour day and we was run out in line of battel and kept so all day and the Yankees crost over the River that day

And the 12 day we was marched around to the left of our armey and was expecting to have to fight every minnet but did not for thar was no fiting don except the pickets and canonading

And the 13 we was marched back to the wright and laid in a line of battel all day under the Yankees shells but non of ous got hurt

And that nite we was sent to the front on picket and laid clost to the enemey all nite and went marching about day we comenced fyring at them and cept it up all day and there was about 15 kild and wounded in our Regt: but non kild in our Company, B. Richmond and P. S. Donahan was slightly wounded and that nite we marched back in the woods And we staid thar all day the next day and at nite we had to bild ous sum brest works

And the next morning which was the 16 General Hood came riding up and said well Boys you all did such great works hear last nite that you scard the Yankees on the other side of the river but we staid thar all day

And the next morning which was the 17 we marched back to our old camps

And the 24 day was cool and cloudy and it was wash day with me.

And the 25 which was Christmas morning was foggy but soon cleard off and was a pritty day but I dident have nothing to drink nor no young ladies to talk too so I seen but little fun

And the 26 was a warm cloudy day and me and M. Walker went to the depot

And the 27 we and Lewis Smith went back to the Depot and after nite I went to the show to see the Monkey.

And the 28 day was clear and warm and Preacher Miller of Company C. preached for ous in the evening and his text was in 126 Psalms and third virse the Text was this The Lord hath done great things for us: Whereof we are glad:

And the 29 day was a prity warm sunshiney day And I was on divishion gard at General Hoods headquarters

And the 30 day was warm and cloudy but no rain

And the 31 day which was the last day of 1862 was cool and cloudy and our Regiment had muster inspection in the day and at nite our Company had to go on picket gard down the bank of the Rapahanok River whar we was in about a hundred yards of the Yankees pickets they was on one side of the river and we was on the other we was in talken distence but our officer would not alow ous to talk they would cum down on the bank and hollow to ous and say if we would bring the boat over that they would come over on our side and have a talk. So that was the last of our works for the year 1862.

BARTLETT Y. MALONE
Co. H. 6th N. C. Regiment

CHAPTER IX

*"We was expecting the Yankees
to cross the River"*

The first day of January was a pritty day and our Company was on picket down on the Rapahanock River about a mile and a half below Fredericksburg Va.

And the 2 day was also a nice one

And also the 3 was a pritty day

And the 4 day was a pritty warm day and we all was on Bregaid inspection the 4th.

And the 5 day was warm and looked like the spring of the year and we was all on Bregaid Drill the 5 day down on the old Battel field.

And the 6 day was cloudy and raind a littel

And the 7 day was clear and cool and we all was in General Revew

And the 8 day was cloudy and cool

And the 9 day was clear and cool and we all was on Divishion revew again General Hood was our revewing officer

And the 10 day was cloudy and raind all day long

And the 11 was cloudy and cool

And the 12 day was a pritty day

And also the 13

And the 14 was warm and cloudy and we built a chimly to our tent today

And the 15 day was warm but very winday and R. H. Wells started home this morning on a furlogh

And the 16 day was a very pritty warm day and we had orders to cook too days rations we was expecting the Yankees to cross the River again but they did not

And the 17 day wa clear but very col indedd:

And the 18 was cool

And the 19 was warm and I was on gard

And the 20 was cloudy and cool

And the 21 was a very cool and raney day,

And also the 22 day was raney and very cool.

And the 23 day was cloudy in the morning and cleared off warm about an hour befour the sun set

And the 24 day was warm and cloudy and the old Bludy 6th and 54 and 56 N. C. Regt was transferrd from the old 3 bregaid which was comanded by General Law (E. M. Law) to the 7 Bregaid which was comanded by General Holk (R. F. Hoke).

And the 25 day was cloudy and raind a littel in the morning about 12 olclock and we got to General Holk (Hoke) Bregaid about 11 oclock which was 15 miles from General Lows (Law's) Bregaid whar we started from:

And the 26 day was warm and cloudy

And the 27 was a very raney day indeed

And when I got up the morning of the 28 it was a snowing and it snowed all day long

And the 29 day was clear and cool and the snow was about 10 inches deep on the ground

And the 30th was clear and cool

And the 31 was pritty and Mr. Mitchel Johnston and Mr. John Evans arrived at our camp today on a visit.

CHAPTER X

"The dark days of Winter . . .
bright days of Spring"

The first day of February which was the Sabath was a pritty spring day

And the 2 day was cloudy and raind in the morning but clear and very windy in the eavning

And the 4 day was cloudy cool and windy

And the 5 day it Snowed in the morning and raind in the eavning

And the 6 day was raney

And the 7 clear and warm

And the 8 day which was the Sabath was a beautyfull spring like day

And the 9 was also prity and

And the 10th day was snowing and also the 11 was

And the 12th was a pretty warm day.

The the 13 was clear and cool.

And the 14th was cool and clear.

And the 15 was warm

And the 16 was warm and clear

And the 17 was a snowey day and we all had to go on picket down at Port Royal.

And the 18th it raind all day long and the snow nearly all melted of by nite and we still stade on picket

And the 19th was cloudy but no rain and we returned to our Regiment

And the 20 was warm and clear

The 21 was warm and clear

The 22 was a very bad day it snowed and the wind blew all day and at nite the snow was about a foot deep.

And the 23 day was warm and clear but the snow dident melt no great deal

And the 24 was warm and General Stokes Bregaid and General Lautons (Lawton?) had a snow ballen

And the 25 was a warm sunshiney day

And the 26 was a raney day and nearley all of the snow was gone by nite.

And the 27 was warm and cloudy and our Brass Ban got back from Richmond.

And the 28 which was the last day of February was coal and cloudy. And Mr. Portland Baley of Company D. 6th Regiment N. C. Troops was shot to death to day at 2 oclock with musketry.

Now the dark days of winter is gon And the bright days of Spring is come.

B. Y. Malone.

CHAPTER XI

"Our men and the Yankees are a fyting"

The first day of March was coal and raney in the morning and in the eavning it was clear and very windy And the 2 day was a beautyfull Spring day.

And the 3 day was a beautyfull one and our Regiment left the old camp clost to Port Royal and marched back clost to Fredericksburg and taken camp again clos to the one we left

The 16 day of March was cloudy and coal And Mr. Stons in Co. F. 57 N. C. Regiment was shot to death to day with musketry.

The 17th of March the Yanks crossed the Raphanock River at Keleys foad and our calvry whipt them back.

And the 20 was cloudy in the morning and snowd a littel in the eavning and Mr. I. H. Compton arived at our camp today on a visit And the 21 it Snowed untell it was about 3 inches deep on the ground

And the 22 the snow all melted off And Mr. Compton and Johnston left camp today for home.

The last day of March the Snow was about 3 inches deep on the ground.

The Month of April (May and June)

The 4 day April was cloudy and coal in the day and after nite it comenced Snowing And the morning of the 5 the Snow was about 3 inches deep on the ground and five companys of our Regt had to go on picket down on the Raphanock River

And the 6 day was clear and warm and the snow nearly all melted of by nite and we still staid on picket and the 7 day we retired to our camps.

The 18 day which was the Sabath was a beautyfull Spring day and General Jacksons preacher preached in our camps and his text was in Hebrews 3 chapter and part of the 7 and 8 virses the words was this: To day if ye will hear his voice harden not your harts.

The 23 day was raney and we had orders about nite to cook too days rations thar was sum few Yankees crossed over the river at Port Royal and taken a wagon or too from our men but they soon went back and our Regt dident have to leave the camp

The 26 day of April which was the Sabath was a beautyfull day And I went to meating at General Jackson

Headquarters And the Preacher taken part of the 16th chapter of Luke commencen at the 18 virse for the foundation of what remarks he made And in the eavning we had preachen in our Regiment from a preacher in the 18th Virginia Regiment. And his text was in Proverbs 18th chapter and the later clause of the 24th virse which reads thus: Thar is a friend that sticketh closter than a brother:

The morning of the 28 befour I got up I herd a horse come threw the camp in a full lope and it was not meney minutes untell the man come back and sais Boys you had better get up we will have a fight hear to reckly and I comenced geting up and befour I got my close on they comenced beating the long roal and and it was not but a minnet or too untill I herd the Adgertent hollow fall in with armes the Reg: then was formed and marched to the Battel field the Yankies comenced crossing the river befour day and by day they had right smart force over the pickets fought sum on the 29 and a good deel of canonading was don and it raind sum in the eavning

The morning of the 30th it was a raning and evry thing was very still untill about twelve oclock it ceased raning about ten o'clock they comenced cannonading and cept it up untill dark

The first morning of May 63 our Regiment had to go in front on picket it was very foggy in the morning but soon got clear as soon as the fog was off we found the

Yankees had a very strong line of Scirmishers in about 5 hundred yards of ours we cood see a great meney Yankees on the other side of the river but we couldent tell how meney was on this side we could hear very hevy canonading up the river in the eavning It is repoted that our men and the Yankees was a fyting at Keleys Foad:

CHAPTER XII

"And General Jackson died to day"

The 2 day of May was a very pritty day and our Regiment was relieved from picket about day and fell back to our brest works again our men fyerd on the Yankies from too Batterys about 10 o'clock and the Yankies returned the fyer from one Battery it was kept up about a hour but no damedge don as I have herd of we can still hear them a fyting at Keley's Foad

And about 5 o'clock in the eavning we could see the Yankees a marchen up on the other side of the river by regiments and most all went back from on this Side of the river and General Earley thought that they was all a going back and taken all of his men but a Louisiana Bregaid and started to reinforce General Lea And about the time we had gone 6 miles they come orders that the Yankees was atvancen again whar we had left And then we had to turn back and march all the way back about 10 o'clock in the nite. And the next morning which was the 3 day our men comenced Buming (bombing) the Yankees and they returned the fyer and ther was right

78

smart canonading and picketing don untell about 12 o'clock and then for sum cause we was all ordered to fall back about a half of a mile to our last breast works but as soon as dark come we marched about 2 miles up the River.

And the next day which was the 4 we was marching about first from one plais to a nother a watching the Yankees untell about a hour by sun and the fight was opend our Bregaid went in and charged about a half of a mile and just befour we got to the Yankee Battery I was slitley wounded above the eye with a peas of a Bumb non was kild in our company. Lieutenant Walker was slitley wounded in the side. I. R. Allred was wounded in the arm hat to have it cut off. I. E. Calmond was slitley wounded in the arm. I. L. Evins had his finger shot off— the fift day we found the Yankees had all gon back on the other side of the River and we marched back down to the old camp ground and taken up camp again.

The 10 day of May which was the second Sunday was a very pretty day and I went to headquarters to preaching and the preachers text was in Romans the 8th chap and 28 virse the words was this: And we know that all things work together for good to them that love God. And General Jackson died to day which is the 10th day of May

The 17 and 18 days was pritty and warm and our Regiment was on picket down on the Raphanoc and the 18th we got back to the camp:

And again the 25th we had to go on picket And the 27 we got back about 12 oclock and in a few minuets after we got back we had to go on a General Revew General R. E. Lea revewed General Earleys Divishion.

The last day of May we had marchen orders and after nite Mr. Tassett preached in our Regt his text was in St. Johns 3 chapt & 16th virse.

The 4th day of June about 11 Oclock in the nite we left our old camp clost to Fredericksburg and marched twar Culpeper and bout 6 O'clock the 5th day we got to Spotsylvaney Coathouse and about 2 o'clock in the eavning we stopt for to camp for the nite after marchen about 20 miles that day And the 6th day we stade in camp untell about 2 O'clock in the eavning for General Hils core was a fiting at Fredericksburg the Yankees crossed ther after they found out that we had left we marched about 8 miles the 6th day and it raind on ous very hard befour we taken up camp.

And the 7th day we started on our march about sun up and about 12 o'clock we waded Rapadan River at Rackoon Foad and about 4 O'clock in the eavning we stopt to camp again in about 5 miles of Culpeper Coathouse.

The 8th day we marched up to Culpeper and stopt to cook Rations The 8 day we staid at Culpeper untell about 3 O'clock in the eavning and then we was ordered down to Brandy Station about 4 miles from Culpeper whar the

Calvry hat bin fiting all day and we staid all nite and the
next morning we found that the Yankees had all gon
back on the other Side of the River and we marched back
to Culpeper again and cooked another days rations and
about 3 O'clock in the eavning we started again in the
direction of Winchester and we got as far as Hasel Run
(Hazel Run or Deep Run) by nite And the next morning
which was the 11th we started about sun up and about
9 O'clock we got to a littel town cauld Woodwin and
whilst we was a passen threw the 6th N. C. Brass Ban plaid
the Bonnie Blew Flag. And about eleven O'clock we got
to a littel town cauld Sperysvill 5 miles from Woodwin
And about 2 O'clock in the eavning we past threw Washington and ther we found a meney pritty and kind Ladies
they had water all along the streets for the Soldiers to
drink and we dident go but a few miles futher untell we
stopt for the nite after going about 20 miles that day.

And the morning of the 12th we started about sun
up and about 3 o'clock in the eavning we crossed over the
Blew Ridg and past threw a littel town cauld Front Royal
and about a mile from thar we waded the Shanadoah
River and taken up camp on the other bank that nite.

And the morning of the 13th we started at day and
when we got in 12 miles of Winchester we found that
the Yankees was at New Town on the Pike road running
from Winchester to Strawsburg (Strasburg) 7 miles from
Winchester and we turnd and went by thar and caught
up with the Yankees about half way from thar to Win-

chester and attacked them and drove them back about a mile by nite

And the next morning which was the 14th General Hooks (Hoke) Bregaid and General Smith and Hases (?) all moved around to the west of Winchester and taken 20 peases of artillery with ous and when we got opersit the Yankees work the artillery taken ther position and about 3 o'clock in the eavning our Baterys opend on them taken them on surprise and General Hases (Hays) and General Smith Bregaid charged on them and taken their first line of brest works befour nite And General Johnstons (Johnson) Divishion was a fiting them on the other Side clost to town

And the next morning which was the 15th the Yankees had left their works and was a trying to make thir escape toward Martinsburg but about day they run up on General Johnstons divishion about 5 miles from town wher three Regt of them was maid to stack thir armes and a grate meney kild and wounded we then marched down to whar Johnston fought them that morning and stopt and staid thar all day

And the next morning about 10 o'clock our Regt was marched back to Winchester for Provost gard and about a hour befour sun down I was sent to Taylor's Hotell with 10 men to gard the Yankees Prisoners And I staid ther the next day and also the next

And the next morning which was the 18th I was relievd about 9 O'clock and started after my Regiment and about 3 o'clock in the eavning we got to Smithfield and by nite we got to a littel plais cauld Leas Town which was 22 miles from Winchester and we staid ther all nite and the next morning we overtaken our Regiment about five miles from thar whar we staid all day

And the next day we staid thar

And the 22th we taken up a line of march again about day and about 7 o'clock we past threw Shepardstown and ther waded the Potomac and landed in Maryland about 8 oclock And about 3 miles from thar we past threw Sharpsburg And about 3 miles from thar we past threw Ketersvill And about 3 miles from thar we past threw Boonesboro and about 3 miles from thar we stopt to camp.

The 23 we left about day and when we had gon about 4 miles we come to Beversvill and about 7 miles from thar we past threw Coverstown And about a mile from thar we past threw Smithburg whar we found a good meney Secesh And about 2 miles from thar we got to a littel town cauld Ringgoal wright whar the line run between M. D. & P. A. And about 2 miles from thar we stopt to camp and cook rations closs to Wainsboro.

The morning of the 24 we left about 7 oclock and after marching about 5 miles we come to a town cauld Quincy And about 3 miles from thar we past threw

Funktown and about 4 miles from ther we got to Greens-wood whar we taken up camp for the nite but our company had to go on gard at a town cauld Faytvill about 2 miles off.

The morning of the 25th I got a Splendid breakfast in Faytville And about 2 Oclock in the eavning we was releaved and went back to the Regt:

And the next morning which was the 26th we had orders to leave at day break but it was a raning so hard we dident leave untell about 8 oclock and it dident Still sease raning but raind all day but we got as far as Momenburg by nite which was 14 miles from whar we left in the morning And our Calvery taken a 135 prisners clost to the littel town

The 27 we left about 6 oclock and after marching about 6 miles we come to a town cauld Hunterstown And about 4 miles from thar we got to New chester And 3 miles from thar we got to Hampton And 3 miles from thar we got to Berlin whar we taken camp for the nite

The 28th we left at sun up and about 12 oclock we got to Yolk which was 12 miles from Berlin:

The 29th we stade at Yolk in the Yankees Hospital.

The 30th we left at day break and taken the same road back that we com And about 12 oclock we got back to Berlin again And when we stopt for nite we was about 20 miles from Yolk:

CHAPTER XIII

Battle of Gatersburg — "We couldent see what we was a doing"

The first morning of July we left earley and about 12 oclock we got to Gatersburg (Gettysburg) which was about 10 miles from whar we started in the morning And when we got thar we found the Yankies was thar And in a few minutes after we got thar we was ordered to the feal Our Bregaid and General Hases (Hays) charged the enemy and soon got them routed and run them threw the town and then we stopt

In our Company George Lyon Marshal Walker and Thomas Richard got kild And Sidney Hensby Anderson Plesant D. A. Walker Garababel Grimstead William Dunervant & Bedford Sawyers was wounded

The 2 day we laid in a line of battel at the Same plais And the enemies picket a firing on us all day Thomas Miles kild on picket Shot in the head And about Sun down our Bregaid and Hases (Hays) was ordered to charge just in frund and take the enemes Batterys we charged and succeeded in driven the infantry

from behind two stone fences and got part of the Batterys
But it was soon so dark and so much smoke that we
couldent see what we was a doing And the enemy got to
geather again and we had no reinforcement and we had
to fall back to our old position Colonel I. E. Avry
(Avery) was kild in the charge in our company non kild
Andrew Thompson Franklin Wells and R. Y. Vaughn
was wounded And Michager Miles misen

The 3 morning we went back in town and laid in a
line of battel all day in the Streets And thar was a great
deel of fiting don that day but our Divishion was not
cauld on

The next morning about a hour befour day we went
back about a mile from town and staid thar all day

The morning of the 5 we left befour day and it a
raining as hard as it could poor and marched in the
direction of Hagerdstown and didnt get but about 6
miles all day for the Yanks calvry cept a running up on
ous all day

And the 6th we left at day and about 2 oclock we
got to Wainsboro and we past threw town and then stopt
to cook rations

The 7th we taken the road to Hagerdstown which
was 10 miles from Wainsboro And about 2 oclock in
the eavning we got thar and taken up camp

The 8th day it raind very hard and we still stade at
the same plais the 8 we staid thar and the 10 we staid at

the same place untill about a hour by sun And then started and past threw town and went about a mile toward Williamsport and stopt and staid all nite

The 11th we taken our position in a peas of woods and after nite built brest works

The 12th we staid behind our works and no fiting don except sum picketing And after nite we was ordered to the wright And was marched down in rear of A. P. Hills old Divishion

The 13th we staid thar untill dark and then started to retreet back across the Potomac And it was about 6 miles to the river and it was a raning very hard And we was a moving all nite and the next morning about sun up we waded the Potomac at Williamsport and it was waist deep And then we marched about 6 miles and stopt to cook rations

The 15th we marched about 7 miles and stopt at nite clost to Martinsburg And the 16th we marched up to Darksvill and stopt again And we still staid at Darksvill untell about a hour by sun and marched to the Alagater mountain by 10 Oclock in the nite:

The 21 we left at day break and crost the mountain And marched as far as Hedgersvill by 2 Oclock in the eavning which was 25 miles we expected to bag the Yankees at plais but when we got thar they was all gon;

The 22th we left Hedgersvill and marched back to Bunkerhill whitch was 18 miles.

The 23 we marched and about 10 oclock we marched threw Winchester and taken the road to Culpeper and marched about 5 miles and stopt for the nite:

The 24th we marched near the Shanadoah River and found that the Yankees had got possession of the gap in the Blew Ridg

And then we taken the write and come into the Winchester and Stanton Road at Middeltown 5 miles from Strawsburg and we stopt at nite clost to Strawsburg which war 23 miles from whar we started at in the morning

The 25th we marched all day toward Stanton and travild about 18 miles and stopt clost to Edensburg:

The 26th we past threw Hawkenstown and 2 miles from thar we come to Mount Jackson and we marched as far as New Market and stopt for the nite

The 27th we left the Stanton road and taken a road that led to Gordensvill: we crost over the Shanadoah mountain and crost the Shanadoah river on Pontoon Bridges and when we stopt at nite we was at the foot of the Blew Ridg which was 18 miles from Newmarket

The 28th we crost over the Blew Ridg which was 14 miles across it

The 29th we marched up to Maderson coathouse whitch was 6 miles and stopt and taken up camp

The 30 we staid at the same plais

The 31st we left at one Oclock and marched down between Culpeper and Gordensvill

CHAPTER XIV

"Our Cavalry had a littel fite in the eavning"

And we staid in camp clost to Rappidan Station untell the 14th of Sept. 63. And the morning of the 14th we was rousted up and gave orders to cook one days rations. And about sun up we started to meat our enemy and we met them at Sumersvill foad on the Rappidan River which was about 5 miles from our old camps. We had not bin there long untell our enemy comenced throwing bumbs amung us but as soon as our Batterys got position and fired a few shots the yanks all left the field. And the 15th we laid in the woods all day. No fiting don but some canonading and picketing but at dark our Reg't went on picket down at the foad. The 16th as soon as lite our men comenced firing at the Yanks and they at us and kept it up all day about 10 o'clock in the day Capt. Pray (or Ray) of Co. D & Lieut Brown of Co. E and 18 men voluntierd and went up the river and crost in a littel Boat and Slipt up to some old houses and fierd at the Yanks & run about 200 of them out of their works and captured a horse severl good Guns Blankets another trick and then crost back and never got a man hirt. They kild 4 or 5 of the Yanks & wounded 4 which they taken prisners. We got 4 wounded in our Reg't. dewing the day. At nite we was relieved by the 57th N. C. Reg't. The 17th no fiting don except a few picket shots evry now an then at the foad.

Evry thing was quiet then untell the 5th day of Oct. 63. And the 5th day of Oct. about tenn Oclock we was ordered to fall in at a moment and then marched to our post and taken our position in a line of battel. And we remaind so untell nite and then was marched back to our camps again. The Yanks could be seen mooving about from a hight on our side of the river. Our Generals surposed that they was agoing to make an efert to cross. But they did not: they was onley moving camps: All was quiert then untell the 8th. The 8th day we left our camps about dark and marched about 2 miles and stopt and staid all nite. The 9th day we marched up to Orange C. H. by 12 o'clock: then taken the road to Maderson C. H. (Madison) marched 6 or 7 miles and stop for nite again.

The 10th we got to Maderson by 4 o'clock in the eavning and crost Roberson River at 3 and then marched about 4 miles futher toward Culpeper and stopt for nite our Cavalry had a littel fite in the eavning at the River taken about one hundred prisners. The 11th we marched toward Culpeper and got in 6 miles and stopt and cooked 3 days rations. it was 20 miles from Maderson C. H. to Culpeper C. H.

The 12th we had orders to leave at 2 o'clock: A. M. but did not leave untell day we marched on then untell we was in 2 miles of Culpeper. And then taken the left and came in the Warrenton road at Pickersvill And thar we waded Haselrun and marched on to the Rappahannock River and campt clost to Warrenton Spring. The 13th we marched up to Warrenton and stopt and cooked 2 days rations: The 14th we left for Bristol but had to drive our enemey befour us our Cavalry was fiting them allday and some times the Infantry, our Divishion don a great deal of hard marchen had to dubbelquick nearly one third of our time. A. P. Hill Corps overtaken the Yanks at Bristol Station and had a littel fite: we did not get thar in time to be ingaged

The 15th the Yanks had all fell back to Sentervill (Centerville) we did not go eney further our Cavalry follerd them and taken severl Prisners.

The 16th we tore up the Railroad

The 17th we staid in camp clost to Bristol Station.

The 18th we left at 3 o'clock in the nite for Rappahannock and got as far as Beattoe Station by nite.

The 18th we marched to the Rappahannock and crost and went in camps between the river and Brandy Station

The 28th our Reg't went on picket on the Rappahannock

The 29th we was relieved

The 30th we had bregaid drill

The 31st had muster inspection

CHAPTER XV

"We was then cutoff and had to Surender"

The 5th day of Nov. General Lea & Goverer Letcher of Va. revewed General Stuart Cavalry clost to our camps

The 6th we was paid off And paid up to the first day of November, 1863.

The 7th about 2 o'clock in the eavning orders came to fall in with armes in a moment that the enemy was advancen. Then we was doubbelquicked down to the river (which was about 5 miles) and crost and formed a line of battel in our works and the yanks was playing on ous with thir Artillery & thir skirmishers a fyring into ous as we formed fyring was kept up then with the Skirmishers untell dark. And about dark the yanks charged on the Louisianna Bregaid which was clost to the Bridg and broke thir lines and got to the Bridge we was then cutoff and had to Surender: was then taken back to the rear and staid thir untell next morning The morn-

92

ing of the 8th we was marched back to Warrenton Junction and got on the cars and about day next morning we got to Washington we then staid in Washington untel 3 o'clock in the eavning of the 8th then was marched down to the Warf and put on the Stemer John Brooks and got to Point Lookout about one O'clock on the eavning of the 10th day of November 1863. The names of the men that was taken prisner when I was belonging to Co. H. was Capt. Lea Lieut. Hill W. H. Bowldin N. W. Hester W. W. Murrie C. Rile H. Malone I. R. Aldridge L. T. Anderson A. I. Brincefield I. E. Covington T. Y. Compton I. C. Chatham T. H. Evans G. R. Grimstead W. A. Hughs N. Hooper H. Kersey A. More W. D. Richmond F. Simpson R. Swift L. Sawers H. Roscoe A. Tucker John Walker W. S. Walker W. F. Wells I. Wren S. Hensley And Segt. A. P. Rudd

Our rations at Point Lookout was 5 crackers and a cup of coffee for Breakfast. And for dinner a small ration of meat 2 crackers three Potatoes and a cup of Soup. Supper we have non. We pay a dollar for 8 crackers or a chew of tobacco for a cracker.

A Yankey shot one of our men the other day wounded him in the head shot him for peepen threw the cracks of the planken

The last day of November was very coal indeed and the Yanks had inspection of ous Rebels. One of the Yankee Sentnerls shot one of our men the other morning he was shot in the head: soon died.

All the wood we get to burn at Point Lookout is one sholder tirn of pine brush every other day for a tent 16 men to every tent

The 16th of Dec. 63 a Yankey Captain shot his Pistel among our men and wounded 5 of them; since one has died—he shot them for crowding arond the gate. The captain's naim that shot was Sids. Him and Captain Patison and Segt. Finegan was the 3 boss men of the prisoners camp.

The 24th of Dec. 63 was a clear day but very cool. And Generl Butler the Yankey beast revewed the prisnors camp:

The 25th was Christmas day and it was clear and cool and I was boath coal and hungry all day onley got a peace of Bread and a cup of coffee for Breakfast and a small Slice of Meat and a cup of Soop and five Crackers for Dinner and Supper I had non:

The 26th was clear and cool and dull for Christmas

The 28th was cloudy and rained a littel The 28th was a raney day.

The 29th was cloudy in the morning and clear in the eavning. And Jeferson Walker died in the morning he belonged to the 57th N. C. Regt. The 30th was a beautyfull day.

The 31st which was the last day of 63 was a raney day. And maby I will never live to see the last day of 64. And thairfour I will try and do better than I have. For what is a man profited if he shal gain the whole world and loose his one Soul: Or what Shal one give in exchange for his Soul:

B. Y. MALONE.

CHAPTER XVI

"Our beds is composed of Sea feathers . . ."

I spent the first day of January 64 at Point Lookout M. D. The morning was plesant but toward eavning the air changed and the nite was very coal. was so coal that five of our men froze to death befour morning. We all suffered a great deal with coal and hunger too of our men was so hungry to day that they caught a Rat and cooked him and eat it. Thir names was Sergt. N. W. Hester & I. E. Covington.

The 6th was coal and cloudy and we had 9 men to die at the Hospital to day. Our beds at this plaice is composed of Sea feathers that is we geather the small stones from the Bay and lye on them

The 7th was very cool a small Snow fell after nite

The 10 was a nice day and I saw the man to day that makes Coffens at this plaice for the Rebels and he sais that 12 men dies here every day that is averidgs 12

The Commander at this point is named Marsto

The 22th day of January 64 was a very pritty day And it was my birth day which maid me 25 years of age I spent the day at Point Lookout. M. D. And I feasted on Crackers and Coffee The two last weeks of January was beautyfull weather

The Month of February. 64 The first day of February was warm but cloudy and Sum rain:

Be content with such things as you have: For he hath said I will never leave thee nor forsake thee So we may boldly say the Lord is my helper and I will not fear what man shall do unto me

There fell a Small Snow the morning of the third Sergt. A. P. Rudd & Gidney King arived at Point Lookout from Washington the 4th. We changed Cook houses on the 7th of Feb.

The 14th of Feb was a pritty day And the Yankes Sirched the Prison Camp the Rebels was all sent out side under gard. And then they sirched and taken evry mans Blanket that had more then one. And taken evry other little trick that the Rebels had. They found too Boats that the Rebs had maid.

375 Officers arived at Point Lookout from Jonstan Isle the 14th of Feb. The Yankey papers say that they are having a Gun maid that weighs 115,000 lbs. 21 ft. long carries a Ball that weighs 1000 Lbs and a shell that weighs 700 lbs.

The 17th it was so coal that we all had to lye down and rap up in our Blankets to keep from freazing for we had no wood to make us a fire.

The 18th it was so coal that a mans breath would freaze on his beard going from the Tent to the Cookhouse. O, it was so coal the 18th

The 20th was pleasant and General Butler the Beast revewed the Prison Camp again for the Second time

The 24th was a beautyfull day And too of the Rebs got kild the nite of the 24th attempting to get away: We was garded at Point Lookout by the second fifth and twelfth Newhampshire Regiments untell the 25th of Feb: And then the 26th N. C. Negro Regiment was plaised gard over ous

A Yankey preacher preached to the Rebels the 26th day of Feb: 1864: His text was in first Corinthian 16 chap and 22th virse The words was this: If any man love not the Lord Jesus Christ let him be Anathema Maren athas That is let him be acursed when the Lord shal come

CHAPTER XVII

"A nother Neagro kild him Self"

The first day of March was coal and raney: And our Company was examined on the Oath question evry man was taken in the House one at a time and examiond: the questions asked me was this: Do you wish to take the Oath and join the U. S. Armey or Navy: or work at govenment work or on Brestworks or Do you wish to take a Parole and go to your home if it be insied of our lines or do you wish to go South I told him I wished to go South: He then asked me my name County State Company & Regiment The 2d two thousen Rebels left Point Lookout M. D. for Dixie:

The 3d I met with The good luck of geting sum Cloathing from Dixie: 600 Rebels left for Dixie again the 9th.

Another boat load of Rebels left Point Lookout the 16th for Dixie.

250 Officers arived at Point Lookout the 20th

One of our Rebel officers maid me a present of a dollar in greenback (the 21st) he stuch it threw the crack of the planken to me without being asked

The 20h of March a Yankey Sergt: named Young shot one of our Officers for jawing him:

The 22d was very coal and stormey and a while befour nite it comenced snowing and snowed all nite: the snow would avridge 3 inches deep the next morning:

The 25th I went to the cookhouse for a cook:

The Month of April

The first day of April was a very nice day.

The 5th was a very bad day it raind hard snowed and the wind blew the Bay was so high that it overflowed part of the Camp. Some men had to leave thir tents and moove up to the Cook house: There was some men in camp who had been going about of nits and cuting tents and sliping mens Knapsacks Hats Boots and Sumetimes, would get Some money They cut into ours and got money and cloathen all amounting to about one hundred dollars: One nite the Negros was on gard and caught them they was then plaised under gard and made ware a Barrel Shirt (and marched) up and down the Streets with large letters on them the letters was this *Tent Cutters*

The 12th the 3d Maryland Negro Regiment was plaisd on gard around the Prison Camp: When the

Negrows first come on gard they wore thir knapsacks and when they was put on poast they puled them off and laid them down at the end of thir lines And Some of our men stole too of them: And when the Negro found it was gone he sais to the next one on post Efrum-Efrum: tell that other Negrow up dar that the white folks has stold my knapsack a redy: The other one sais they have stold mine too but I want caring for the knapsack all I hate about it is loosing Sophys Garotipe (daguerreotype?) One day too of them was on poast in the Streets and met up at the end of thir lines and comenced fooling with thir Guns what they cauld plaing bayonets they had thir guns cocked preseantly one of thir guns went of and shot the other one threw the brest he fell dead: the other one sais: Jim, Jim get up from dar you are not hurt your just trying to fool me:

The nite of the 18th a negrow Senternel shot one of our men wounded him very bad threw the sholdier

The nite of the 21st a Negro shot in a tent wounded two of our men

The 27th a load of Sick Rebels left Point Lookout M. D. for Dixie.

The 29th a nother Neagro kild him Self. Shot him Self in the mouth with his gun:

The Month of May 64

The 3d day of May 6 hundred Rebels left this plaice for Dixie

The 13th about one hundred prisnors was brought to this pliace they was capturd clost to Petersburg Va.

The 15th 40 prisnors arived at this point captured between Richmond and Petersburg by Gen. Butlers armey

The 17th about one thousin Prisnors arived at this plaice was captured at the wilderness The 17th about 1000 was brought in from General Leas armey

The 18th four hundred more was brought in the camp

The 24th a Neagro Senternal Shot a mung our men kild one and wounded three it is thought that one of the wounded will die:

The 28 four hundred more prisnors arived here We have Pork and Been Soop to day for dinner Will have beef and Coffee to morrow I believe I will go down in Camp, but the sun is very hot

CHAPTER XVIII

"General Grant and General Lea are fiting"

The first day of June was clear and hot

The 4th We had Beef and Potato Soop for dinner the Yanks are not a going to give us no more Coffee and Sugar from this on

The 8th 6 hundred Prisnors arived at this point from General Leas Armey

The 10th we have Old Bacon to day for dinner for the first time sience we have bin at P.t. Lookout

The 11th 500 more prisnors arived here.

The 18th of June which was three years from the time I voluntierd was cloudy and cool. And we had Pork and Hominy for dinner There is some talk of moving the Prisnors from this point it is getting to be very sickley here 11 men died at the Hospital yestiday it is said that the water is not healthy

It is reported that General Grant and General Lea are fiting on the South of the James River

From the 20th of June untell the last was very dry and dusty And we would hear good news evry now and then from our Armey Our Rations Still remain Small

July the 1st 1864

The first day of July 1861 I left home And the first day of July 1862 I was in the fight of Malvin Hill And the first day of July 1863 I was in the fight at Gettersburg And today whitch is the first day of July 1864 I am at Point Lookout M. d. It is very plesant to day We had pical Pork for breakfast this morning and for dinner we will have Been Soop

The 4th day of July was a beautyfull day And the Yanks had thir Vesels riged off with flags they had about 34 flags on each Gun Boat about 12 O'clock they fierd Saluts boath from thir land Batry and Gun Boats.

The 13th day of July 13 of our men died at the Hospital And it was repoted that General Ewel was a fiting at Washington And that our Cavalry was in 4 miles of this plaice the Yanks was hurried up sent in all Detailes at 2 O'clock in the eavning and run thir Artilry out in frunt of the Block house and plaised it in position The 14th 500 Rebels taken the Oath and went outside

The last day of July was the Sabath

Bartlett Yancey Malone

No man is bornd without falts

Too much of one thing is good for nothin

Cut your Coat accorden to your cloth

All are not Sants who go to Chirch

All are not theavs that dogs bark at

Keep your mouth shut and your eyes open

A clean glove often hids a dirty hand

Seay what is well and do what is better

He that will steal a pin will steal a better thing

Fear no man and do justice to all men

Evry Cook praises his own stew

Before thou marry be sure of a house wherein to tarry

Evry bodys business is no body's business

Do what you ought come what may

Love cover meney falts.

The race is not always to the swift nor the battel to the
strong

You cannot catch old birds with chaff.

A bad workman quarrels with his tools

B. Y. MALONE

A Puzzel

There is a thing in divers of countrys
It neither is land nor Sea
It in all sorts of timber
And not in eny tree
It is neither in Italy
But in Rome
It appears twist in evry moment
And not once in twenty years

B. Y. Malone Owes   cts
Q. T. Anderson   Paid
A. P. Rudd   Paid
T. Y. Compton   Paid
Sergt W. T. Johnson
Sergt. Laffoan
Samuel Mothers head
George Anthony

Dew B. Y. Malone
Thomas Murray $1.00
John Forast $1.00
W. A. Hughs $1.00
E. W. Rudd $1.00
N. W. Hester   Paid $5.00
W. R. Richmond   Paid $5.00
T. Y. Compton   Paid $5.00

W. F. Wells	Paid	$5.00
A. I. Brincfield	Paid	$5.00
L. Kersey	Paid	$5.00
B. Y. Malone	Owes	
Q. T. Anderson	Paid	$6.50
A. P. Rudd	Paid	$5.00

Bartlett Y. Malone, Soldier of Co. H. 6th N. C. Regiment.

This April the 16th 64

Point Lookout, M. D.

O, that mine eyes might closed be
To what becomes me not to see
That deafness might possess mine ear
To what concerns me not to hear.

B. Y. Malones Chirography.

CHAPTER XIX

"And I have not got eney Shoes"

The first day of August was clear and very hot And 700 Rebels left here for Some other new Prison to day A mung them was my Brother A. A.

The 2d day of August I wrote home

The 6th of the month there rose a thunder cloud early in the morning and raind very hard: there was a whirlwind just out sid of the Prison on the point it blew the Comasary house and Shop down and seven other Buildings it distroyed a good deal wounded four sentinels broak ones leg There was but littel wind inside of the Prison

The knight of the 7th A Neagro Sentinel Shot one of our men and kild him for no cause attall

The 28th of August a Senternel shot a nother one of our men wounded him very badly it is thought that he will die

The two last days of August cool and plesant

The Month of September

The firs days of September was plesant the Knights was cool but the days was plesant

The 2d day this is And our Rations gets no better we get half a loaf of Bread a day a smal slice of Pork or Beef or Sault Beef for Breakfast for Dinner a cup of Been Soup and Supper we get non Mr. A. Morgan of South Carolina has a vacon Cook House which he has bin teaching School in evry Sience last Spring he is a Christian man he preaches evry Sunday and has prayers evry morning befour School we have a Preacher to evry Division in the Camp Mr. Carrol preaches to our Divi which is the 8th This is the 5th day of the month and we are going to have Been Soup with onions in it to day for dinner we will have Potatoes and Onions boath to morrow the Dr had them sent in here for rebs to se if they would not stop Scirvy My health is very good to day which is the 6th of Sept. 64. But I cannot tell how long it will remain so. for it a raning and very coal to day Aand I have not got eney Shoes

This is the 7th and a pritty day it is and I am laying flat on my back on T. Y. Comptons Bead in Co. G 8th Division Point Lookout M. D.

The 8th was a beautyfull day And I had my Bunk Seting out by the Side of the Cook house and about dark I wanted to bring it in as I had bin doing but the Neagro Sentinel would not let me cross his line So I went down threw the house and asked a nother one if I could cross his line and get my Bunk and he Said yes so I cross and got my Bunk and the first Neagro did not see me. And when he found that the Bunk was gone he come to the house door and wanted to know where that man was that taken that Bunk And if he dident bring it back that he would come in there and Shoot him So then I had to go to the dor and he told me to bring that Bead back So I taken it back and could not get it any more untell I went and got the Lieut. of the Comisery to get it for me So you See this is the way we was treated by the Neagrows. B. Y. M.

The 15th of Sept was a beautyfull day And a general Stir among the Rebs the Dr. was getting up a load of Convalesant men to Send to Dixie. You could See men going to the Hospital to be examiond Some on Cruches and Some was not able to walk and would be Swinging a round others necks draging a long

They got a load of five hundred and Sent them out of the Prison we Surpose they will leave the 15th for Dixie The 19th received a Box of tobacco from my Father James B. Malone who resides in Caswell County North Carolina The 21st all Prisnors belonging to the Confederate Staits Navy was Parold at this place.

This Sunday the 25th of September and it is very coal I wrote home to day

The 26th 800 Prisnors arived at this point belonging to Erleys (Early) Comand captured clost to Winchester The knight of 26th Some one stold 5.45 in greenback from me

The 27th 500 more Prisnors arived here from the same Comand

The 28th the Yanks brought in three Negrows that they caught helping a Lady across the Potomac Some where be tween here and Washington they brought them here and put them in Prison because they would not take the oath

The 30th I wrote to Bro. James

CHAPTER XX

"Christmas day . . . . nothing Strong to drink"

The first day of October was cold and raney day The 3d 800 Prisnors arived here from Early's command captured at Fishers Hill Va. among them was James M Wells of Co H 6th N. C. Regt

The 4th 100 more Prisnors com in Ther is about 10,000 Prisnors here at this time last Summer ther was 15,000 here but Some was sent to Elmira N. Y.

The 7th was fasting and prayer day with ous for the reliece of all Prisnors

Today is the 8th and is very cold

The 13th was very cool And in the eavning 200 Rebs taken the Oath

The 15th I Sold the last of my Tobacco the Box brought me fifty five dollars and 70 cts

To day is the 16th And a beautyfull Sabath it is: the Boys in camp are all in a line wating to be inspected by Major A. G. Brady Provost Marshall

To day is the 18th and Secretary Stanton has just past threw the Camp.

The 21st 200 Rebels arived here from the Valey captured Severl days ago.

The 24th they parold Severl Sick men Said to be 2000 to leave in a few days.

The 25th Some more prisnors come in from the Valey Said that 900 was capturd when they was

The 29th About 80 Rebs arived here they was captured clost Petersburg Old Butler kept them at work on a Pond 8 days under the fire of our guns.

The 31st 600 more Rebs arived here capturd clost to Petersburg

November 1864

The first of November was pritty weather.

The 7th whitch was just twelve months from the time I was captured was a raney day.

The 8th was election day for president Abraham Lincoln & George B. McClellan was candidates

The 9th was warm and cloudy and our Rations ar not a good as they was a year ago: And I See no chance for marching Soon.

B. Y. MALONE.

The 18th of Nov. was a cold raney day Our men are not dying here like they have bin they onley avridge about too a day now The last of Nov. was pritty warm weather

December 1864

The first day of Dec was warm as Spring And the Yanks comenced building some littel plank houses covered with clouth for the Rebs to stay in

The 3d I paid 10 cets to go into a Concert that the Rebs had got up in camp it was a very good thing they performed in a vacon Cook-house.

The 4th which was the Sabath I went to meating at the School house Mr. Morgan lectured on the Parable of the Sower & in the eavning I was at the Same plaise and Mr. Carol preached a good Surmond from the later clause of the 2 virse 7 chapter of Amos: Theas was the words: By whom Shall Jacob arise: for he is small. After preaching was over the Sunday School classes met and thir teachers taken up the balance of the day in asking them questions and explaning the Scriptures to them We have white gard now for patroles in camp of knights the Neagros got so mean that the General would not alow them in Side of the Prison they got so when they would catch any of the men out Side of thir tents after taps they would make them doubble quick or jump on thir backs and ride them and some times they would make them get down on this knees and prey to God that they might have thir freadom and that his Soul might be sent to hell

114

To day is the 15th and it is cold looks very mutch like Snow we have had very coald weather for the last week we get Split Peas now to make Soups. Some day we get Bacon and some days Picle Pork and fresh Beef once a week

My health is very good at this time I weigh 155 lbs We have comenced drawing wood we get two smawl shoulder turns a day to a Company Each Company has 100 men

The 21st was a very cold raney day Brigadeer General Barnes in comand of the Point A. G. Brady is Provost Marchall Capt Barnes assistant Prov.

The 24th was a beautyfull day I chopt wood in the morning at the cookhouse in the eavning I bought 3 apples and set in the Sun Shine by the Side of Sergt. A. P. Rudd tent & eat them. And then my Self Q. T. Anderson W. W. Murrie & W. F. Wells went up to the School house to a Debate but did not get in And then we went back to the Tent and found T. Y. Compton with a newspaper that he had bought and we spent the remainder of the day in reading it.

The 25th was Christmas day And a beautyfull one it was. But I had nothing Strong to drink and but little to eat I had Some loaf Bread fryed Meat & Corn Coffee for breakfast and for dinner I had a cup of Split Pea Soup.

In the eavning I went to the School house to meating Mr. Carrol preached his text was in Zachariah 15th chapt

7 virse After preaching I went to the Comiseary and found that Mr. Walas had bet Mr. Barby five dollars that there was a man in Camp that could eat 5 lbs of Bacon and 3 Loafs of Bread each loaf weighing 2 lbs at one meal. When I left he had onley about $1/4$ of a pound of Bacon and a half of a loaf of bread they Said he eat it all befour he quit. This man belonged to the 11th Ala: Regiment

The 26th was a raney day

The 27 & 28 was cloudy

The 29th was cold and cloudy & Snowed a little in the Eavning

The 30th was cold

The 31st was very cold and Snowed a littel evry now & then threw the day.

CHAPTER XXI

Home and the End

The first day of January was very cold & the grown was coverd with Snow:

The 2d was cold and cloudy

The 3d it snowed a littel in the eavning

The 4th was very cold and the Snow was 3 inches deep

The 5th was warm and cloudy

The 6th my Self A. R. Moore James R. Aldridg Nathaniel Hooper & T. Y. Compton built us a hous out of cracker Boxes the house coust us $8.80 cts we bought a stove from the Sutlar the Stove coust us $8.00 the Stove and house totel $16.80.

The 15th was a beautyful Sabath & I went to meating & Mr. Newman preached from Psalms 8 ch. 4th Virse

The 17th it Snowed in the morning And about one thousen old men & littel Boys left for *Dixie.*

117

The 21st it rained and Sleated all day & a large Dixie mail came in one hudred & Sixty dollars worth of Due Letters:

The 22d was cold and cloudy & it was my birthday whitch made me 26 years old. And about 600 prysnors come in to day captured at Foat Fisher The men that came in Say that General Whiten & Colonel Lamb was captured and also wounded After knight a Neagrow Sentnal Shot one of our men and kild him.

The 23d a large Dixie mail come in I got 2 letters from home & one from Bro. Jim.

The 28th was clear but the coldest day we have had this winter there was a man froze to death in the 5th Division after knight.

The 29th was the Sabath I went to meating with Mr. Athy preached

The 30th & 31st was pritty warm days.

February 1865

The first of Feb. was warm And 500 Rebels come in captured clost Atlanta Ga.

The 4th all men belonging to Kentuckey Missouri Louisina Tennasee & Arkansas was cauld to go to *Dixie*.

They Still cauld on the 5 & 6th.

The 17th all prisnors captured at Gettersburg was cauld out.

The 18th the Gettersburg Prisnors left for *Dixie.*

The 21st all Prisnor capturd at Rappahanoc Station was cauld we all went out and Signed the Parole and was put in the Parole Camp and staid there most all the 24th then we was put on the Steamer George Leary we got to Fortress Monroe about dark And then run as far as Hampton Roads and there we staid all night Started next morning at light which was the 25 got to Acorns Landing about 10 oclock which was about 12 miles from Richmond on the James River we then marched from there to Camp Lea we got to Camp Lea about dark We then Staid at Camp Lea untell the 27 when we wen over to Camp Winder.

March 1865

The 2 day of March I got my Furlough the 3 they paid me 12 months wages which was 237.00.

Went down to Richmond got on the cars about 6 O'clock in the Eavning

The 4th I got to Barksdale Depot about 10 in the morning, got off at Barksdale marched to the Road house by dark Eat Supper with Mr. Hanrick marched on 2 miles further and Staid all night with Mr. Moss. Left early next morning which was the 5th eat Breakfast at Mr. Maxtons got home about 1 O'clock in the Eavning.

B. Y. MALONE.

LAST ENTRY

B. Y. Malone was borned in the year of our Lord 1838 rased and graduated in the Corn field & Tobacco patch And inlisted in the war June the 18th 1861 And was a member of the Caswell Boys which was comanded by Capt Mitchel And 25 was attatched to the 6th N. C. Regt. which was comd by Coln Fisher who got kiled at the first Manassas fight which was fought July the 21st 1861. They was comanded by W. D. Pender untell the Seven Pine fight which was fought the 30th day of May 62 Col. Pender then was promoted to Brigadier General Then Capt. I. E. Avry of Co. E. was promoted to Lieut Colonel who comanded untell the Battel of Gettysburg where he was kild which fought the 2d day of July 1863.

Major R. F. Webb was then promoted to Col. who comanded untell we was done at the Rapahanock Bridg the 7th of Nov. 1863. Our Regt when was captured belonged to General Hooks Brigard Earlys Division Ewels Corps Leas Armey.

B. Y. MALONE.

APPENDIX

A LIST OF CO. H*

Sargants.

1 Johnston I. H.
2 Rudd A. P.
3 Bauldin W. H.

4 Hester N. W.
5 Malone B. Y.

Corpral

1 Murrie W. W.
2 Biele C.

3 Walker M. H.
4 Tompson A. J.

Privat

1 Aldridg I. H.
2 Anderson Q. T.
3 Alred J. B.
4 Bivins M
5 Brincefield A. J.
6 Brankin I
7 Boswell T
8 Cooper W. H.
9 Covington I. E.
10 Compton I. E.
11 Colmond J. E.
12 Cape T. H.
13 Chatham C

14 Donoho S.
15 Dunervant I.
16 Dunervant W.
17 Evins T. H.
18 Enoch R. H.
19 Fauller I
20 Fitch G. S.
21 Grimsteard G.
22 Hensley S
23 Hensley A
24 Huges W. A.
25 Hooper N
26 Johnston I. H.

*This roster of Malone's company appeared in the diary following entry of July 31, 1863.

27 Kersey L.

28 King S

29 Lyon G.

30 Lyon I. H.

31 Loyd I. W.

32 Lewis C.

33 Miles M.

34 Miles T. C.

35 Miles J. S.

36 Moore A.

37 Malone H.

38 Murrey T

39 McKinnie Murphy B. P.

40 Mosey J. W.

41 Oliver J. S.

42 Olver T

43 Plesant A. M.

44 Page F.

45 Roberson J.

46 Rudd E.

47 Richmond W.

48 Richmond T.

49 Rigan N.

50 Simpson F.

51 Swift R.

52 Smith L.

53 Swift H. A.

54 Stadler G.

55 Subfield R.

56 Snips J. C.

57 Tucker A.

58 Vaughn R. Y.

59 Williams J. W.

60 Williams J. R.

61 Walker John

62 Walker W. S.

63 Walker J. H.

64 Walker D. A.

65 Walker W. T.

66 Wells M.

67 Wells W. F.

68 Wren W.

MALONE'S DICTIONARY

(first page)

Predestination: the unchangerabel purpose of God
Ordain: To appoint; to invest
Foreordain: to ordain beforehand
Centurion: a Roman officer over 100 men
Need: to want
Nephew: a Brother's or Sister's child
Tares: A kind of wild peas
Wait: to tarry
Weight: heaviness
Wear: to carry as clothen
Ware: Merchandise
Wast: to spread
Waist: a part of the body
Foul: filthy
Fowl: a bird
By: near at hand
Buy: to purchase
Consort: husband or wife
Concert: harmony
Disease: sickness

(Second page)

Candidate: one who seeks an office
Caliber: the diameter of a gun bariel
Arsenal: a magazine of military stores
Assailant: one who attacks or invades
Armada: a fleet of armed ships
Amulet: a charm worn about the neck
Amazon: a female warrior
Simile: a comparison
Nudity: nakedness
Oration: a public speech
Penury: poverty
Erelong: before a long time
Erenow: before this time
Meager: lean thin poor
Kill: to slay
Lain: did lie
Wrote: did write
Too: likewise
Two: twice one
Decease: death

INDEX

Acorns Landing, 119
Alagater Mountain, 87
Aldie, 62
Aldridge, I. R., 93
Aldridg, James R., 117
Allred, I. R., 79
Anderson, L. T., 93
Anderson, O. T., 115
Ashland, 49, 50, 57, 60, 61
Athy, Mr., 118
Avry, Colonel I. E., (Avery), 86

Baines, Brig. Gen., 115
Balden Green, 49
Balden, Mr., 34
Baley, Mr. Portland, 73
Baltimore, Md., (see Baultimore)
Barby, Mr., 116
Barksdale Depot, 119
Baultimore, 62
Beattoe Station, 91
Berlin, 84
Berrysville, 62, 63
Beversvill, 83
Blew Ridg, 57, 62, 81, 88
Blue Ridge Mountains (see Blew Ridg)
Bombings (see "Bumbings")
Bonnie Blew Flag, 81
Boonesboro, 83
Bowldin, W. H., 93
Brady, Major A. G., 112, 115
Brandy Station, 80, 91
Brass Ban (band of 6th N.C. Regt.), 73, 81
Brincefield, A. I., 45, 93
Bristol, 81
Bristol Station, 91
Brown, Lieut., 89
Brother Albert, 45, 46

Brother James, 111
Bucktown, 63
"Bumbings," 58, 59, 78, 87
Bunkerhill, 87
Butler, Gen. Ben, 94, 98, 102, 113

Calmond, I. E., 79
Camp Barton, 47, 49
Camp Fisher, 47
Camp Lea, 119
Camp Winder, 119
Casualties, 52, 53, 58, 59, 66, 73, 74, 79, 82, 85, 86, 90, 98
Caswell Co., N.C., 110
Cedar Run (see Sedar Run)
Centerville (see Senterville)
Charlestown, 63
Charlottesville (see Sharlottsvill)
Chatham, I. C., 93
Chickahominy River, 55, 56, 58
Colchester, 45
Cold Harbor, 58
Colmond, James, 48
Compton, I. H., 60, 74, 75
Compton, I. T., 31
Compton, S. F., 32
Compton, T. Y., 93, 109, 115
Cousin Anderson, 36
Couvington, Sergt., 34
Coverstown, 83
Covington, I. E., 93, 96
Culpeper, 64, 65, 80, 88, 89, 90, 91
Culpeper Coathouse (Courthouse), 62, 80, 90

Darksvill, 87
Diversions, concert in cookhouse, 114; debate, 115; meating in schoolhouse, 115; monkey show, 67; playing, 34; rabbit hunting, 32; snow bawling, 35, 73

127

Index

129

Yankees, 45, 53, 54, 55, 58, 60, 66, 67, 68, 74, 75, 76, 77, 78, 79, 81, 82, 85, 86, 87, 88, 89, 90, 91, 92, 93, 97
Yankey Beast (see Butler, Gen. Ben)
Yanks (see Yankees)
Yolk, 84

Yolktown (Yorktown), 48, 50, 52
York (see Yolk)
York River Railroad, 58
Yorktown (see Yolktown)
Young, Mr., 33
Young, Sergt., 100

And the enemies picket a'
firing on us all day. Thomas
Miles was kild on picket Shot
in the head And a bout
Sun down our Brigoid and
Hoses was orderd to charge just
in frund and tdie the enemes
Battergs we chorged and succeeded in driven the infentry from
behind two Stone fences and
get part of the Batterys But it was
Soon So dark and So much
Smoke That we couldent See
what we was a doing And
the enemey got to geather a
goin and we had no Renfoe-
ment and we had to fall back.
To our old peritien—
Colonel S. E. Avery was kild
in the charge in one Compay
non kild Andrew Tompson